UNCHARTED TERRITORY

NAVIGATING SPIRITUALLY ON YOUR JOURNEY THROUGH COLLEGE

NATASHA JESSUP

All scripture references are from the King James (KJV), New International (NIV), New Living Translation (NLT), Message (MSG), and Amplified (AMP) versions of the Bible.

ISBN-10:0-9984116-3-9
ISBN-13:978-0-9984116-3-7

JessUP Media, LLC
P.O. Box 501892
Indianapolis, IN 46250

www.jessupfromhere.com

They say it takes a village to raise a child. With that being said, I would like to dedicate my first book to MY VILLAGE. I especially want to dedicate this book to those of my village who have gone on to be with The Lord: my late grandparents, Mildred & John Hawkins, Lady D.E.G, and my Purdue Angel. In good and bad, the word that comes to mind for each of them is FAITHFULNESS!

Table of Contents

Acknowledgments

It would only be fitting that I first acknowledge the head of my life, My Lord and Savior, Jesus Christ. Without Him, I am nothing. You using a mere vessel like me is beyond words. I am forever grateful and can truly attest to the fact that when nothing else could help, Your LOVE lifted me.

To my parents, Stephanie and Marcus Jessup, I am immensely BLESSED to have you two as parents. Thank you for raising me in the way that I was to go; I can honestly say that it has not departed from me. Mommy, I could write a book about you. The example you set of keeping God first has not gone unnoticed. Thank you for being my #1 fan and for always pushing me to be PURPOSE DRIVEN. Daddy, you were few in words, but your presence in my life has made more of an impact than you know. I can always count on you to be there for me. Your actions truly speak louder than your words and for that, I'm grateful. Again, thank you both and I love you!

To my brother, Marcus Jr., where do I begin? If no one else believes in me, I know you do. Whenever I need motivation to keep pushing, I can always look to you. As I have stated before you are one of my biggest inspirations. You have shown exemplary strength and tenacity in the way that you pursue your God-given purpose. I am thankful that God entrusted me to be your big sister. I am and will forever be my Brother's Keeper, love you Bubby.

To the best grandparents on this side of heaven, Myrtle and Joe Humphries and Will Morris…the majority of the reason I am considered an old soul. All of my grandparents have meant the world to me, but I have been able to glean from you three for 25 years now; God is good! Myrtle Lee (don't be mad LOL), thank you for always going above and beyond concerning me. You probably didn't think I was listening, but I heard every word to every lesson you have ever taught me. I know it was some of your prayers in particular that have brought me through. I would be remiss if I didn't acknowledge my great-grandmother, Edna Williams, who God has allowed to see what will be 92 years. Your faithfulness to God is nothing short of amazing, and I'm glad I have been able to witness His faithfulness towards you.

Lastly, to my spiritual covering, Bishop Lambert Gates Sr. Thank you for heeding to the spirit for the things concerning my life in particular. Every time you have spoken into my life, it has only confirmed what God had already affirmed, so again I say, thank you!

The Journey

"What has been will be again, what has been done will be done again; there is nothing new under the sun" (Ecclesiastes 1:9, NIV). This means that the experiences you feel that you monopolize, someone else has already experienced them. Before going off to college I made the mistake of telling God that I felt like I had not really been through anything, so I have a few experiences to share. Yes, these are my college experiences. And yes, a lot of the content is directed towards college students or those on their way, but the principles apply to everyone, no matter what path of life you are on.

I've noticed that as young people of God we either do one of three things. We either get to college and go the straight and narrow, conform to the world around us and put God on hold until we graduate, if then, or we attempt to do both.

So often I hear young people say, "Well, being saved can be so boring." It is often said that life is what you make it. If you don't like something it is up to you to change it. Being a Christian does not exempt you from the earthly pleasures God has made available to you. But it is our responsibility to seek Him for direction and not be partakers of temptations that are not acceptable to God. I will talk more about this later in the book, but I just want to personally let somebody know that it is possible to be a Christian, go away to college, and still have FUN!!!

We are all called to be servants, to help others. The church does not elaborate much about education, or more so the challenges we would encounter entering college as a Christian. No one I knew, attending or who had completed college really warned me about what I was to expect "spiritually."

In writing this book, I am also being obedient to the Holy Spirit. This is NOT a tell all book nor a book to detour you from your walk with God, just some of my college experiences as they relate to certain topics and how I personally, with God as my source, was able to take advantage of the resources He made available to me to accomplish and remain focused and be victorious in my quest to remain in His Will. If I can influence my peers by being transparent, I am ready to be the vessel that God can use.

My prayer is that this book helps others to be better prepared for college all around, but especially spiritually. The reason I said "spiritually" is because the majority of the time this is where we as young people of God fall short when we go off to college.

Introduction

So you're going away to college, for many it is the first time you are out on your own, without your parent(s) or guardian breathing down your neck about what you should or shouldn't do. You now feel like you have this sense of freedom to be and do whatever you want. So, what do you do? It's almost like the question where it asks if you could commit any crime and get away with it what would it be. Although not as extreme, many young people (especially those in church) approach college with this mindset…as if college is a four-year pass to throw all morals out of the window.

Righteousness means to do what is morally just or to live a life that is pleasing to God. Life is all about choices. Depending on the path you choose, some choices may push you closer in your relationship with Christ while others push you further away. Mary had to make a choice with her alabaster box. She was obedient when directed to anoint Jesus' feet with her best perfume. Although criticized, Mary did what was 'right' in God's eyes.

College will bring about choices that you may have never had to decide on up until now, such as a major or discipline to go into, where to live, which roommates to live with, what organizations to join, etc. We who proclaim to be Christians are called to be 'set apart' from the rest of the world. The only way we can do that is by following the example of Jesus Christ.

If you choose to wholeheartedly follow Christ you will be misunderstood, you may lose some friends; you will be talked about and criticized. In spite of everything that will come against you, the best choice you will ever make is following Jesus Christ.

The next few chapters are examples of my choices that were made during college, some good some bad, both resulting in consequences. I don't think I would change any of the choices I made because they were learning experiences, which have afforded me the opportunity to share with you.

It is often said that college is the place where young people 'find themselves.' What I want you to understand is that if you seek Christ and allow Him to control every aspect of your life, down to the choices you make; you won't have to use these four years to find yourself like the rest of the students on campus, He'll begin to show you who you are and the plan He has for your life.

This is not a book of rights and wrongs, and you will not always get it right. This is a book to motivate you to continue striving for righteousness even after you fall. Although it may seem like no one is watching, the truth of the matter is that God is always watching. Don't get caught up in the superficial pleasures of what college or life has to offer.

"If serving the Lord seems undesirable to you, then choose for yourselves this day, whom you will serve" *(Joshua 24:15, NIV).* **Choose wisely**

It's Necessary

You've made it to one of the most important chapters in this whole book. I thought I'd put it at the beginning for anyone like myself, who struggles to finish tasks.

Before you begin, I want to ask you these questions: **What is the Holy Spirit and what do you expect from it? Do you know when God is speaking to you? How often are you in the Spirit?** If you don't already know the answers to these questions, then hopefully you will have a better idea or understanding by the end of this chapter.

So it was freshman year of college. It never failed, I always had a spirit of frustration, most of the time it didn't show but sometimes it did. I had this feeling of emptiness inside like a part of me was missing which didn't quite make sense because I had the Spirit of God dwelling on the inside of me. I would read my Bible, fast sometimes and pray all the time but my praying felt more like a monolog. Then my praying began to be prayers of frustration towards God, asking Him if He was listening to me and why He wasn't speaking back to me. I would always ask Him how He expected me to do everything according to His Will if He wasn't giving me any direction. I felt completely LOST!!!

Of course, there was no problem with God's line of communication, the problem was obviously me. Those years before I went off to college I had only allowed myself to hear God through other people, whether it be my pastor, family members, friends, other ministers, etc. But now I was at a place where there was no one there but God and I, and I had to literally learn how to hear the voice of God for myself. *"Anyone with ears to hear must listen to the Spirit and understand what he is saying to the churches" (Revelation 2:29, NLT).*

At first the idea of learning to hear God's voice made me a bit nervous, I didn't want to say I heard God's voice but then it really ended up being my own self-conscience, but that was all a part of recognizing or discerning His voice.

- The Holy Spirit -

In order to be led by the Holy Spirit, you have to discern the voice of the Spirit, not with the natural ear but the spiritual ear. In order to discern the voice of the Spirit, you should probably know a little bit about the Spirit. First and foremost, the Spirit is a person. It dwells in us and will do so forever in eternity.

One of the relationships we have with the Holy Spirit is a personal relationship; and the Spirit not only has a personal relationship with us but with the Father and Son as well. By having a relationship with the Father and Son, the Holy Spirit is able to intercede for us.

God speaks to each of us differently. A lot of times we hear people talking about a still small voice, but that's not always the case for everyone and what He has to say is not always something deep like a lot of people think it is. I will never forget, this one night I took a study break to get some dinner at this Chinese restaurant on campus and the Spirit spoke to me. I didn't know it at the time, but the Spirit was telling me to check my order before I left. I can't necessarily explain it, but there was like this strong tugging in my spirit telling me to make sure my order was correct. Of course, I'm thinking I've been to this place a million times and they have never gotten my order wrong before. I'm sure you can figure out the rest, I get back to my apartment and come to find out that I had the wrong order. There was another time where I had gone to the mall between classes to exchange a pair of jeans, again, I had that tugging in my spirit to check and make sure I had the correct item. You would think that I would have learned from the first time, but apparently I hadn't because somehow I ended up with the very pair of jeans I went in to exchange. Unfortunately, these were not the only times I ignored the Spirit, it took me some time, but I know now. So be patient, it might take you some time, but you will get there.

Just as the Son of Man is God, the Holy Spirit is also God. When the Spirit is speaking to you, God is speaking to you; so when you ignore the Spirit, you are also ignoring God. God is a spirit so when we talk or pray to Him it's essential that we also be in the spirit. *"God is a Spirit: and they that worship him must worship him in spirit and in truth" (John 4:24, KJV).*

It is imperative that you be in the spirit at all times so you can hear The Spirit tell you what is yet to come through your college journey and in life. For those of you from a church background, when I say be in The Spirit at all times I don't mean going around speaking in tongues all the time. Being in the spirit all the time means being prayerful, listening for that voice of guidance that only comes from the Holy Spirit.

- Praying in the Spirit -

The Spirit knows us better than we know ourselves; therefore being able to pray for those things our physical minds don't know to pray for. In return, the Spirit speaks only what He hears and guides us into truth.

It wasn't until recently that I found out just how important praying in the spirit is. My mind is always wandering, especially when I'm praying. Prayer already pleasures your spirit, but when you pray in the spirit, your spirit is more stimulated to hear the voice of God by His Spirit.

Praying in the Spirit is meant to show love and affection towards God, and it is not to be understood by man. When you pray in the Spirit, you are more accessible to hear the voice of the Lord because your mind is yielding to the Spirit.

The voice of the Holy Spirit will always point to Jesus, so if you are struggling to figure out if it is God speaking to you, then really listen to the voice and figure out if it is bringing glory to Jesus Christ. That voice should not only glorify Jesus, but it should be true to the Word of God.

So now you're probably wondering, what does that have anything to do with my college journey? Believe it or not it has a lot to do it. As you continue to read you will see more topics that dwell more on the natural side of college life but in the midst, things are still working out spiritually. Like the saying, the devil meant it for evil, but God meant it for good. Things might be going wrong in your natural life, but spiritually, everything is working out for your good. You might not understand what I'm talking about now but keep reading and as another saying goes; you will understand it better by and by.

Money is NOT the Motive

*Turn my heart toward your statues and not toward
selfish gain. (Psalms 119:36, NIV)*

For as long as I can remember I had always wanted to
be an architect. My junior year of high school I
received my first internship at a civil engineering firm.
Being outside all day taking notes versus sitting in a cold
office in front of a computer was like heaven on earth at
that age. It was one of the best summers of my life. As
the internship was coming to a close, I was asked
questions about my future plans and I was saying how I
wanted to pursue architecture. It was then that I was
persuaded that architecture was "okay and all," but as a
civil engineer you're basically doing the same thing as an
architect except you're making more MONEY! Like any
logical person at that age would do, I eventually decided
on civil engineering as my major, soon to find out that,
that was one of the worst decisions I had ever made.

We as young people get so caught up in preparing for
college in other areas of our life, forgetting we need to
include God in everything that we do. Not once did I ask
God if engineering was what I was supposed to be
majoring in because I was so focused on the money I
would be making once I became an engineer. This brings
me to my next questions: **Have you asked God if that's
the college you're supposed to be going to? Have you**

6

even asked Him what you're supposed to be majoring in, or more importantly, what His Will is for your life?

I had it all figured out, I would get this engineering degree, take the fundamental engineering exam my senior year so that I could practice being an engineer, using the money to pay off my student loans, and then work four years and take another engineering exam so that I could be a professional civil engineer.

Problem number one, notice I used "I" four times. I was sitting there trying to figure things out for myself, but God had already worked it out, according to His Will. *"I have it all planned out—plans to take care of you, not abandon you, plans to give you the future you hope for" (Jeremiah 29:11, MSG).*

The second problem was that engineering was not at all what I wanted to do, nor was it what I had a passion for, I was simply trying to please others. Still thinking about the money, I got to a point where I would say, "I don't want to be an engineer I just want the degree." Engineering literally made me miserable. I spent so much time complaining about the work, I wasn't giving it my all, so my grades began to drop, on top of other things. So my grades are dropping, on account of that I'm retaking classes, retaking classes means more time in college and everybody knows time equals money, so I was just digging myself into a deeper hole, all because I wanted to make decent money when I graduated.

When you place value on something you begin to focus on that thing more, and the more focus you give that thing, the less focus you give to God. It doesn't necessarily have to be money, but in my particular situation it was. In Matthew 6:24, we are told that no one can serve two masters because you will hate one and love the other. You cannot serve God and deceitful riches, money, possessions, or whatever is trusted in. **What thing have you given a value that is taking your focus off of God?**

- The Root of All Evil -

"For the love of money is a root of all kinds of evil. Some people, eager for money, have wandered from the faith and pierced themselves with many griefs" (1 Timothy 6:10 NIV).

I believe that if I were not so grounded in my faith or my relationship with God, I would be able to attest to this verse in particular. Junior year of college I got myself into a situation, not necessarily because I "love" money but because I wanted to save some money. Notice I said, "I got myself into a situation," often times we want to blame the enemy for everything when really in some cases it is ourselves we should be placing blame on, but that is another story. It is not that money is evil, it is more so the love and focus put towards it that is; the accumulation of it is a major distraction.

Sophomore year was coming to a close and my roommate and I were determined that we were not staying in dorms again, but we needed two more roommates so we could get an apartment and save more money. We already knew where we wanted to stay, but we really did not know two other females who had not already signed a lease for an apartment, and we definitely did not want the apartments to just give us anybody.

The apartments were having a signing incentive where if we signed our lease within the next two weeks the entire signing fee would be waived. Long story short I took care of the situation and we made the deadline. I felt like a big load had been lifted off of me, but that was only the beginning.

Up until that point, I had been praying to God to send us some roommates, and I thought He had, but something still was not sitting well with me; sign number 1. The night before our offer was accepted, I remember my late grandmother telling me to keep praying because I did not want to rush these kinds of things; sign number 2. I moved in the following semester and come to find out I would be living in an environment that was not conducive to my lifestyle or suitable for my liking. This just goes to show you should probably know every little thing about people you decide to live with before you make a big decision like I did. Believe me; it will make your life a whole lot easier.

The Spirit of God has a way of not only telling you about good things to come but warning you of bad things as well. That something that was not sitting well with me was no other than the Spirit and not only was He speaking to me, trying to warn me, He also spoke through my grandmother. Because I was disobedient to the Spirit, I now had to go through a year of being exposed to a very negative environment all because I wanted to "save some money."

- The Money Will Follow -

At one point in time, I wanted a place to myself, but after looking at the prices to stay by myself, I thought that was a bit too expensive for me. I realized that I had trusted God with little things in my life but when it came to getting money for an apartment I had put a limit on Him.

I read in a book that money is anywhere you really want to be. If you have a desire to do something and it is in the Will of God, then it has come to pass. For example, there is a lack of money for you starting your own business, if it is meant to happen, in His timing, God will supply the funds and everything else you need to start that business. Don't stress!

Many times people associate being successful with having money but that is not necessarily the case for everyone, and as you go through life your definition may change. My definition of success is being able to help others no matter where they are in life and it may very well mean something different to someone else. Do not get so wrapped up in making money or having money that you forget about Who supplies you with the money.

Some of the unhappiest people in the world are those who possessively "have it all." A lot of times, they accumulate all of their possessions because they're trying to fill a void that only Jesus Christ himself can fill. Mark 10:17, talks about the rich man who followed all of the commandments but when asked to forfeit all of his riches to the poor and follow Jesus, the rich man refused. **Would you be willing to give up everything to follow Jesus?** If you are aware that your struggle is covetousness, pray and ask God to detour your focus from vain or worthless things and onto the love of things valuable to Christ.

Circle of Life

A man that hath friends must shew himself friendly: and there is a friend that sticketh closer than a brother. (Proverbs 18:24 KJV).

Relationships are key to success and life. Jesus said to love your neighbor as thyself, but it doesn't mean you have to have a relationship with everyone. Love is more of a feeling or affection towards, while a relationship is a connection or association with. You have to distinguish the difference between your friends who last a lifetime and your associates and enemies who may be there for a season, seasons or a lifetime.

I have my church friends, high school friends, my college friends, and my family friends. Although I met my friends at different walks in my life, I have always been the same person around each of them. There are so many reasons why I call them my friends, but I would say the main reasons are that they stand for me; they respect what I believe; and no matter where we are or what we go through we will always remain friends, continually lifting each other up.

One of my friends from high school and I did not really speak until senior year of high school and we did not become as close as we are today until freshman year in college. I believe I was going through one of my depressed episodes and I was homesick. I guess the Lord had laid it on her heart to text me and just check to see how I was doing. I ended up telling her what was going on and she asked if she could pray for me, so I obliged. She called me up and prayed one of the most powerful prayers; I remember it like it was yesterday. Next thing I know the tears began to flow, she finished the prayer and ended the phone call with I love you and that was truly the beginning of our lifetime friendship.

When you are down, a friend is someone who will pray for you when you can't even pray for yourself. Nothing is more effective on earth against the evil works of the enemy than an agreement between two or more people. *"Two people are better off than one, for they can help each other succeed. If one person falls, the other can reach out and help. But someone who falls alone is in real trouble" (Ecclesiastes 4:9-12 NLT).*

Do a reevaluation. Who are those people you call "friends"? People have a tendency to rub off on others they are close to. **Do your friends lift you up or do they just bring you down? What kind of friend are you to others?**

- Guilty by Association -

Associates! Those people you might confuse with friends. Those people who could be in your life for a season, seasons or a lifetime. Those people you only hear from when they want or need something. Those people who tend to believe what you do but don't necessarily stand for you. Those people who can rub off on you in a positive and/or negative way. They are not your friends, but they are not necessarily your enemies either. ***"Become wise by walking with the wise; hang out with fools and watch your life fall to pieces" (Proverbs 13:20 MSG).***

The Spirit has a way of revealing yourself to you. If you know who you are in Christ but you tend to change who you are when you get around certain groups of people, those are what you call associates or acquaintances.

Your associates are those people you find pressuring you to do things that go against what you stand for, and these just won't be people outside of church but in church as well.

A great majority of my associates consist of people I met in college. I was cordial with them; I could hold a conversation with them on any given day, hung out with them from time to time, did homework together, etc. When it came time for them to drink and smoke and go partying that is where I drew the line. Anyone I associate with, especially those at school, know I love them, but they also knew that I was not about that lifestyle. I didn't drink or smoke because I thought I was better than them, again, those are just two things that are not conducive to my spiritual beliefs.

We should not judge people who do those things, we should pray for them; who are we to judge because at one point in time we were right there along with them. As many say, life is all about choices; but at some point in your walk with Christ, you have to choose between those people who help you strengthen your walk with Christ and those who will help you tear it down.

14

"Do not be unequally yoked with unbelievers [do not make mismated alliances with them or come under a different yoke with them, inconsistent with your faith]. For what partnership has right living *and* right standing with God with iniquity *and* lawlessness? Or how can light have fellowship with darkness?" (2 Corinthians 6:14, AMP). We often throw this verse at couples where only one partner is living a life for Christ, but this applies to any relationship.

- Love Your Enemies -

Enemies! Everybody has at least one and that is the devil himself. "The LORD said unto my Lord, Sit thou at my right hand, until I make thine enemies thy footstool" Psalm 110:1. You've got to learn to, "Use your Footstools." Things that come up against you; those circumstances that are intended to bring you down, use those to get you to your next level in Christ. For example, you may have some friends who will turn their back on you but instead of being upset thank the Lord for allowing them in your life for that season because everything happens for a reason and then thank God for Him never turning His back on you.

I have a friend whose boss was constantly on her case for no reason, but instead of arguing with her boss or talking about her she went to work every day with a positive attitude, prayed for the job God had blessed her with and prayed for that boss. Her boss was eventually transferred to another department.

Your enemies have no control of you or what you do because God has already prepared the way for you. In 1 Peter 5:8 the Bible talks about Satan prowling around like a roaring lion seeking someone to devour. Satan tricks people into submitting to sin and fear because he has become a master at hurting those who fear him or who aren't ready for him. We must be reminded that God is the creator of all things and the devil is mad because he can't create anything; he can only twist good things God has created.

Earlier, I talked about living in an environment that was contrary to everything I believed, because I was trying to save some money. All first semester I would vent to my mom about the situation, and I would pray and fast about my situation, but it seemed like nothing was changing. I came back after winter break and before classes even started; the smoking had already begun. I did my usual routine and vented to my mom about it. About a week later I was watching a sermon and the speaker said something like, "instead of talking about them, pray for them." I felt like that word was directed towards me because the whole time I was talking about them and only praying about my situation. That night, I did what the speaker said and prayed for my roommates; after that I promise you, I never smelled smoke in my room ever again. Side note: it's funny how the very One that can take care of our situation(s) is often times the one we go to as our last resort, but that's a conversation for another time. I knew the smoking was still going on because I had to pass through a common area to get to my room one time and I didn't smell a thing once I closed my door. No, I didn't have a ventilator or an air purifier in my room. It was just another one of those things I believe God blocked in my life.

16

If you're actively seeking God, feeding daily on His truth, and walking in the Spirit, your enemy's abilities are restricted. *"Resist the devil and he will flee from you. Draw near to God and He will draw near to you" (James 4:7-8 KJV).* You draw near to God by praying, fasting, reading, understanding, and applying His Word. Many times we are reading The Word, but we either don't understand it, we don't apply it, or both.

It would only be right for me to end this section with one of my favorite scriptures, but don't just read it, ponder on it, try to actually understand what it means; when you do, it will go a long way.

"Love your enemies, bless those who curse you, do good to those who hate you, pray for those who persecute you; In that way, you will be acting as true children of God" Matthew 5:44-45.

- Mentored to Mentor -

Every day you wake up is a learning experience. Yes, you're at school every day getting an education, but in the midst of your natural learning, you must also tend to your spiritual needs. There are many ways to tend to your needs spiritually, but right now I want to talk to you about mentors.

I believe it is essential for young people especially to have mentors. Notice I said mentors with an "s." You should have a natural or educational mentor and a spiritual mentor and however many other mentors you would like. The reason you should have more than one is because mentors can teach you different things from their individual experiences and if you have more than one, you can communicate with each of them on strictly an academic level or on a strictly spiritual level. I'm not saying you can never talk to your spiritual mentor about anything academic or vice versa, but you have that option if you choose to.

So what is a mentor for? In my opinion, a mentor is a teacher, someone who has your best interest in mind; they want nothing more than to see you succeed. They've been in your shoes and they share their experiences to motivate you but at the same time to keep you from making the same mistakes that they made. In the spiritual sense, it is someone who can intercede for you in prayer, someone who can answer questions you may have about the Word of God, someone who is just an example of what it means and looks like to have a relationship with Jesus Christ.

I have been blessed to have two academic mentors that just so happen to have spiritual lives. I've heard both of their testimonies more so about college and they've watched me go through mine but when I would go to speak with them it was pretty much on an academic basis. Although we spoke on an academic basis I knew that they were praying for me, there was even an instance where we all prayed together so I could get some direction from God pertaining to my education.

God has a way of setting you up with just the right people for you to get exactly what you need. One of my mentors had to have surgery because she had an encounter with cancer for the second time in her life. It was a long recovery, but throughout the whole process updates were given through Facebook on her wellbeing just about every day. In the midst of everything my mentor was going through she was still praising and worshipping God.

She had taught me something from a different city and in a hospital room. At the time it seemed like all I was doing was complaining about everything that was going on in my life. I would get on Facebook every day to see what had been posted and it seemed like a spirit of repentance had come over me because here she was sitting up in the hospital after a major surgery STILL praising and worshipping and I was complaining about little things that really didn't even matter. That right there is a true example of what a mentor is and should be. **Do you have a mentor?** If not, pray for God to send you one.

The information or lessons that you take from someone can't just stop with you. As I stated before, we were all called to serve and help others, so use what you've learned to help somebody else. Life is about living and learning. My grandmother has given me many lectures from her life experiences but right after she's done lecturing she always tells me, "I'm telling you this because I don't want you to make the same mistakes I did; I want you to do better." That is the exact same attitude we all should have for one another, to see others do better and not make the same mistakes we've made.

I'm no longer a mentor directly, but I carry myself as though I am because I know people are watching, more so my little brother and cousins. You can't tell someone else to do something if you aren't doing it. For instance, you can't tell someone to stop smoking or drinking if you yourself are still doing those things because they just might be doing it because they see you doing it. I'm pretty sure they have a name for people like that...a hypocrite.

It is said that one must be the change they want to see. You'd be surprised by just how many people are watching you. Many times they are watching you because they see something in you that they want to see in themselves. Do yourself and them a favor by giving them something positive they can take away.

Heart of Temptation

Drugs! Alcohol! Sex! I see these words as a means for people; young people especially, to fit in with the rest of the world or to fill a void that only God can fill. These are just a few but in this day and time, I feel safe to add partying or clubbing and social media (technology in general) to this list, amongst other things.

God gives us choices and I believe one of the hardest choices, as young people, is choosing between wholeheartedly following and serving God or following the crowd (world), our peers. I know personally that you cannot do both, there is no in between.

I'm not really going to go into detail about drugs and drinking and sex, but I do want to leave you with a few verses from 1 Corinthians 6 to meditate on.

"Don't you realize that this is not the way to live? Unjust people who don't care about God will not be joining in his kingdom. Those who use and abuse each other, use and abuse sex, use and abuse the earth and everything in it, don't qualify as citizens in God's kingdom. A number of you know from experience what I'm talking about, for not so long ago you were on that list. Since then, you've been cleaned up and given a fresh start by Jesus, our Master, our Messiah, and by our God present in us, the Spirit. Just because something is technically legal doesn't mean that it's spiritually appropriate. If I went around doing whatever I thought I could get by with, I'd

be a slave to my whims. You know the old saying, 'First you eat to live, and then you live to eat?' Well, it may be true that the body is only a temporary thing, but that's no excuse for stuffing your body with food, or indulging it with sex. Since the Master honors you with a body, honor him with your body" 1 Corinthians 6:9-13 (MSG).

I can't go into detail about drugs, drinking, and having sex because those weren't really my struggle, but I did, however, struggle with pornography. I thought that as long as I wasn't having sex, I wasn't hurting anyone; but that was not the case at all, I was hurting myself. Matthew 6:22-23 talks about the eye being the lamp of the body. I wouldn't say that I was addicted, but I will say that I have seen my fair share. I could pass by guys on campus and mentally undress them or be sitting in class listening to a lecture and dirty images would come to mind; I had corrupted the light on the inside of me. So you're probably wondering how I got over it. I finally got to a point where I was tired of the guilt. Each time I watched I'd tell God it was my last time, but He knew the truth. That's the great thing about God, no matter how many times you fall, He's right there to pick you back up. I'm not proud of this season of my life, but it has allowed me to relate to others who struggle with this same situation. Let God turn your test into a testimony.

I know it's sometimes harder for new believers to flee from temptation because they see or hear about people in church doing the same things they did in the world, but you can't base your choices off of what you may see church people do because they'll be accountable for their own actions. This is why it is so important to get an understanding of God's Word and have a relationship with him for yourself so that you'll recognize tempting people and situations. The Bible says to write God's commandment on your heart, or to know His teachings so that if you find yourself in a tempting situation, you'll know what to do.

I'm not saying you will never be tempted because even Jesus Christ himself was tempted, but we can use that as an example for resisting temptation. For those who don't know the story, you can find it in Matthew 4:1-11, but I'll briefly explain it.

Jesus was led into the wilderness by the Spirit to be tempted by the devil. He had been fasting and praying for forty days and nights to prepare for this test, and the devil told him to turn some stones into loaves of bread, but Jesus quoted the scripture, "man shall not live by bread alone but by the Word of God." Then the devil took Jesus on top of a temple and told him to jump, quoting Psalm 91: "He has placed you in the care of angels. They will catch you so that you won't so much as stub your toe on a stone." So Jesus quoted another scripture, "thou shalt not tempt the Lord thy God. So the devil tempts Jesus one last time on top of a mountain, showing him all the kingdoms of the world saying if Jesus would bow down and worship him, he could have it all. Jesus told the devil to flee and quoted one last scripture, "thou shalt worship the Lord thy God and him only shalt thou serve." Then after the devil had fled, angels came and tended to Jesus' needs.

So if you're like me, you probably have some questions or you may have noticed a few things about this story. I know a question I had when I first read this was: why would the Spirit (who is supposed to lead and guide you in the right direction) lead Jesus to the wilderness knowing he would be tested. It was revealed to me that Jesus was lead there so that God's Word would be fulfilled and to show that you will be tested but also that we'd know what to do when we come into a tempting situation.

We also see that Jesus had been fasting for forty days and nights to prepare for this test from the devil. Sometimes you will have to pray more than usual, fast more than usual, and get into God's Word more than usual. Often times we wait until we're already going through something to look for help and guidance from the Lord.

You might also notice from the story that the devil was quoting scripture, and that is because the devil himself was once an angel so he knows the scripture. You might also notice as I said in the last chapter that the devil twisted God's words and that is why it is essential for us as people of God to know and understand the Word so we can know the truth for ourselves.

You also may have noticed that the devil spoke to Jesus and he didn't stop tempting him after one time, he tempted him three times. We are no better than Jesus, so we will be tempted on many occasions, but we also have to be ready to rebuttal it like Jesus did as well. Don't ever be afraid to talk back to the enemy and let him know just exactly whom he's up against.

One last thing you may have noticed is that after the devil had fled, the angels of God came and took care of Jesus. Every single temptation or test you face is an opportunity for victory. Just remember there is always something for you to look forward to, something better waiting for you on the other side of your test.

I'm human, so I know how hard it is to resist temptation, but then I stepped back and asked myself; "How often did I lead myself into temptation where I knew I'd be tempted to disobey God?" For me, the answer was too often, especially with me being away at school, with no parents. Again, we must not forget that God is always watching.

God understands the devil is tempting you from every angle and he has already promised us that he won't allow us to be tempted beyond our measure. But when tempted he'll always make a way of escape. I heard someone say, "many times your way of escape is usually through a door," whether it is at a party, in a car, or even a bedroom. I want you to do like I did and ask yourself, **"How often do you lead yourself into situations where you know you'll be tempted to disobey God?"**

*"Flee youthful lust; but pursue righteousness, faith, love, and peace with those who call on the Lord out of a **PURE HEART**" (2 Timothy 2:22, KJV).*

- When You Know Better You Do Better -

Don't copy the behavior and customs of this world, but let God transform you into a new person by changing the way you think. Then you will learn to know God's will for you, which is good and pleasing and perfect. (Romans 12:2).

When you get to a point where you're falling into temptation on purpose, it's called presumptuous sinning. It is a state of not caring whether you sin or not because you know God will forgive you. Doing so is dangerous and nothing but a path of destruction you let yourself get into because the Bible says there is no such thing as actually being overcome by temptation. When you continue to purposely sin that's like having no respect or no fear of God and the Bible says, God confides in those who fear him.

You can't possibly inherit the promises of God if you have no reverence of the one who gives you the promise; that makes no sense whatsoever. That's like going to your boss and telling them to give you a promotion, but you never do your work or anything else they ask you to do. Proverbs 1:7 tells us that, "the fear of the Lord is the beginning of knowledge."

I do want to briefly talk about partying or clubbing because for some reason young people don't think they should be included in this category of tempting situations. I've had my fair share of party invites and you might feel like you're missing something but believe me, you're not.

It's not partying in itself, but it's what you're doing or what's being done at certain parties. Some parties are okay, after all the ultimate party is in heaven. Even Jesus himself went to parties, but he went with the ulterior motive of saving souls. *"Jesus, overhearing, shot back, 'Who needs a doctor: the healthy or the sick? I'm here inviting the sin-sick, not the spiritually-fit'" (Mark 2:17, MSG).*

26

Before you decide to go to a party, first ask yourself, **"What are your motives for going to that party?"** Are you going to help others or to hinder yourself? There are so many other activities to partake in outside of partying, get creative. Go to the movies, bowling, rock climbing, laser tagging, putt putting, go carting; the possibilities are endless. Have your own gathering at home, invite some people over, have a movie night, play some games, the list goes on and on. There's this notion that Christians don't have fun, but that's not true there is such a thing as good, clean fun.

Just remember we know not the day or the hour when the Lord will return. We must keep our eyes on the prize and not get distracted by the temporary pleasures of this world. Portray a lifestyle that is pleasing to God. You don't want to be one of those people that God will say He never knew because you knew what was right, but you decided to live your life however you wanted to. Like the heading says, "When you know better, you do better." *"Do not be conformed to this world, but be ye transformed by the renewing of your mind" (Romans 12:2).*

Spiritual Mind Games

Freshman year! My grades weren't where I wanted them to be, I was tired, depressed, homesick, I felt like nobody understood me, I prayed but it felt like God was not hearing or responding to me, I was on the verge of giving up on God and getting ready to do what I wanted to do. I had gone from being a high honor roll student all throughout high school to a college freshman who had seen nothing but D's in math, which just so happened to be my favorite subject. I did what I thought was studying, I prayed, I even fasted, but it seemed like nothing was working. I would always say college sure has a way of making you feel dumb. I had begun to take on some of the effects of depression like sleeping all the time, not eating much, looking angry all the time, and not talking to anybody. While I wasn't talking to anyone the enemy was busy talking to me, just constantly feeding me lies.

I was sitting up one evening waiting for an exam score to be posted and I was really anxious because I had studied like never before and that was the first time I had prayed right before I started taking the exam. My score finally came up and it was a **D**, which was to be my second one that semester and I just had it made up in my mind that with two D's on two exams for that class there was no way I would pass it that semester. I was frustrated and completely hurt on the inside. After that I cried myself to sleep. I woke up that same night still frustrated, still angry, and my crying had become dry tears. I don't know

28

what it is, but there's nothing like pain on the inside. The enemy spoke to me that night saying, "where's your god now?" Then he said, "I know how you can get rid of that pain." I will admit I've contemplated the idea of suicide, but I would never have the guts. I would always say to myself why "live in hell" and then die and go to hell, so suicide was never really a plausible option for me.

Let's PAUSE right here for a minute. For those of you who have never struggled with depression or contemplating suicide you are probably thinking, "all of this over grades." Of course not! This moment was just the end result of things that had already accumulated in my life at the time. It's one of those things you can't fully understand unless you've been there. Okay, now back to our regularly scheduled program.

I listened to the devil that night about getting rid of my pain on the inside and the next thing I knew I was picking up a razor. I started on the outside crest of my eye and ran it down my face representing tears, after that I cut FML (F*** my life) in my left forearm. Now I was not only hurt on the outside, I was still hurt on the inside. This was not because of school still, but because I had fallen into the tricks of the enemy.

It was then I had actually heard the Lord remind me of 1 Corinthians 6:19, *"Do you not know that your body is the temple (the very sanctuary) of the Holy Spirit Who lives within you, Whom you have received [as a Gift] from God? You are not your own."*

I was so focused on God "not" hearing me, responding or helping me that I forgot His Spirit was dwelling inside of me all along. I was not only hurting myself, but I was hurting His spirit as well. I may have been filled with the Holy Spirit back in high school, but it wasn't until that night in my freshman year of college that I began a genuinely *personal* relationship with the Lord and Savior Jesus Christ.

I cried myself to sleep the rest of that night with tears of joy because the Spirit of the Lord had just consumed me and it was one of the best feelings I had felt in a long time. Come to find out the grade that was posted for the second exam was incorrect, and I had really ended up with a B on it. That's just a testimony of how my God worked then, and how He's working even now.

- Spiritual War -

"For our struggle is not against flesh and blood, but against the rulers, against the authorities, against the powers of this dark world and against the spiritual forces of evil in the heavenly realms" (Ephesians 6:12, NIV).

It is quite evident that the devil has been very busy when it comes to young people, college students especially. There have been more campus shootings, more students going missing, and more suicides or contemplating of suicide in college students than ever before.

I read that the devil attempts to make us do five things. He tries to plant doubt inside of us, making us question God's Word and his mercy towards us. He also tries to discourage us, making us look at our problems instead of looking to God for help. He uses diversion, making those things that are wrong for us seem more attractive than the right things. Another tactic is defeat, making us feel like a failure so that we don't even try. Lastly, he tries to delay us, making us put off doing something so that it never gets done.

I'm pretty sure I'm not alone when I say I've become subject to each and every one of these schemes and they've become far too familiar. The problem doesn't come when we fall for his plans it's when we know we're in them, but we don't do anything about it.

I had never told anyone that the devil himself had me contemplating suicide because that's all it was, contemplation. Even in the midst of writing this book, he wanted to make me think I had nothing to live for. Even though I knew I would never do it, my mind stayed in that state for a long time, not because I didn't know what to do but because I let myself stay in that state of mind.

A few people had confirmed what God had already told me concerning my future, so I don't know why I even entertained the devil and his mind games. As I said earlier, a lot of times we blame the enemy for the things we go through or the things that happen to us but sometimes it's just as much our fault as it is his.

I had stopped praying and reading my bible for some weeks, and fasting wasn't even a thought anymore. All the things I knew I was supposed to do to get me out of this position, I completely threw out of the window. It's different when you're on the outside looking in, but when you yourself are going through something like this it's a challenge, believe me.

So you're wondering if it was such a deep state how in the world did I get out of it. I would have to say there were three things in particular: My circle of life, the fear of God and a thing we Christians call spiritual warfare. A lot of people don't like to talk about spiritual warfare, but it was one of the few things that got me through college.

We as children of God can't fight our battles against the devil like we would another person because he is also a spirit. *"For the weapons of our warfare are not carnal, but mighty through God to the pulling down of strong holds" (2 Corinthians 10:4, KJV).* Even though the devil is a spirit he doesn't understand us when we speak to God in our spiritual tongue, he only understands what we say with our natural tongue. That's why it's so imperative that we watch what we say because the devil is listening to every word we speak good and bad.

When it comes to spiritual warfare, we must use the **Armor of God**. "Wherefore take unto you the whole armor of God, that ye may be able to withstand in the evil day, and having done all, to stand" Ephesians 6:13.

"Stand therefore, having your loins **girt about with truth**, and having on the **breastplate of righteousness**" Ephesians 6:14. The girt or belt of truth is somewhat like a tool belt, that supports our lives with the truth of God. God's righteousness is our breastplate of protection; it's only effective when we're doing what's *right* in God's eyes, obeying his commandments, so it should be worn at all times.

"And your feet shod with the preparation of the **gospel of peace**" Ephesians 6:15. The gospel of peace serves as your shoes to stand firmly against the enemy, sharing the Word of God through the works of Jesus Christ.

"Above all, taking the **shield of faith**, wherewith ye shall be able to quench all the fiery darts of the wicked" Ephesians 6:16. Our faith operates all of our other weapons and allows the power of God to protect us from the attacks of the devil.

"And take the **helmet of salvation**, and the **sword of the Spirit**, which is the word of God" Ephesians 6:17. The helmet protects the most vulnerable part of our body, our head. We know we already have salvation through Jesus Christ, so the helmet of salvation is for reassurance. The sword is our offensive weapon; it holds the power of God's Word and the name of Jesus Christ.

Through prayer we have the strength of God. Never take the attacks of the enemy personal because he's not after you personally, he's after the anointing, the calling and purpose you have in your life, and he wants nothing more than to destroy the Will of God.

So you know the tactics of the devil and you know what to do to protect yourself, but I want to leave you with these two verses one last time. *"Finally my brethren, be strong in the Lord, and in the power of His might. Put on the whole armour of God, that ye may be able to stand against the wiles of the devil," (Ephesians 6:10-11, KJV).*

God Can't Use You Sitting Down

There were many mornings where my mom would come in my room, waking me up yelling, "get up from there [bed] God can't use you sitting down. I didn't pay much attention to her then because I was too busy trying to fall back asleep but now that I look back I've grasped the different aspects of what she was really saying or yelling in my case.

We all will be held accountable for what we do and don't do when it comes to God's purpose for our life. The Bible tells us as believers to be the salt and light of the world.

"Let me tell you why you are here. You're here to be salt-seasoning that brings out the God-flavors of this earth. If you lose your saltiness, how will people taste godliness? You've lost your usefulness and will end up in the garbage" (Matthew 5:13, MSG).

We have an obligation to not only spread the love of God but to let it be seen through us as well. *"Let your light so shine before men, that they may see your good works, and glorify your Father which is in heaven" (Matthew 5:16, KJV).* What I'm really trying to say is, get involved. Find some Christian organizations on your campus to join and if there aren't any, start one yourself. And you don't necessarily have to just join Christian organizations because when you're walking in the Spirit

34

people will see something different in you without you even mentioning anything about your faith.

I joined my Habitat for Humanity organization at school. When joining I had no idea that it was faith based, it was just something I had always wanted to be a part of. Little did I know the first time we went out building, we said a prayer; I was surprised but so excited at the same time. You'd be surprised at some of the places you end up and some of the people you affect when you take heed to the voice of the Spirit.

You should never be ashamed or afraid to spread the Word of God. What the Holy Spirit gives us is the power to tell the world about Jesus everywhere we go, Acts 1:8. There is also no reason you should ever feel like you're not good enough. The great thing about Jesus is that he chose normal people to do his work. Matthew was a tax collector; Peter, James, and John were fishermen.

A spiritual gift is every Christian's God-given ability to carry out his function in the body of Christ. Paul talks about at least two gifts all believers have, "a seal of ownership to show who our Master is and the Holy Spirit as a guarantee that we belong to him" 2 Corinthians 1:21-22. Each member of the body of Christ is equally important; if a part is taken away, the whole body becomes less effective. If you don't use the gifts God has given you, the body as a whole will be less effective.

Just think, perhaps there is someone on your campus or job or in your life who will only know about Christ from you or through you. Don't worry; the Spirit will speak and be bold for you. Peter denied Jesus three times before he received the Spirit but after he did he went all around preaching the gospel of Jesus Christ. *"For unto whomsoever much is given, of him shall be much required..." (Luke 12:48, KJV).*

- The Prayer Closet -

You're away at college with a new environment along with new people. You're probably going to want to find a campus church. This was an area I struggled with for the longest because I was only an hour away from home so I would just go to my own church or if not, just watch services via the web. My mom made a big deal about me watching services via the web and I didn't understand the severity of it until later.

We don't just go to church to hear a word from the Lord; it's a place of worship, a place of healing and deliverance. We also go there to share our faith and strengthen each other in the Lord. There may be someone there who's struggling with something in their life, and you could be just that person to help get them through because perhaps you've already been through what they're going through.

Even in his perfection, Jesus still managed to get to the synagogue every week (Luke 4:16) so there should be no excuse why we shouldn't either.

Although going to the physical church is essential, there are going to be some times when you just feel like being isolated from everything and everybody. There will also be some times where you're going to want to be around others, but God isolates you from them so that He can have your full, undivided attention. These will be the times you'll want to go to a little place many call the prayer closet.

"But when you pray, go into your room, close the door and pray to your Father, who is unseen. Then your Father, who sees what is done in secret, will reward you" (Matthew 6:6, NIV).

Your prayer closet doesn't necessarily have to be a closet, although it can be, it doesn't have to be a room period; Jesus went to the wilderness to pray (Luke 5:16). While I was away at school, my prayer closet was my car. And, it doesn't have to be just for prayer either. It can be a place where you can pray, worship, or perhaps just bask in the presence of the Lord. There were many times when I'd be overwhelmed and I'd just get in my car and get lost outside of campus just riding around communing with God, singing, praising and worshipping.

Your prayer closet is usually a quiet place where there is no one there but you and God, the foundation upon where your relationship with Him is built. Just like any relationship, it takes communication from everyone involved. Ultimately that's all that prayer is, communication. You talk, you listen, you get some direction, and you get everything you need in your times of prayer.

Jesus talks about people who pray out in public to be seen and how being seen will be the only reward those people get (Matthew 6:5). Praying isn't a hard thing to do, but then again it should be taken very seriously.

When you pray, don't just repeat what you've heard other people say and don't repeat yourself either because God hears you and to be honest, He already knows what you need before you even open your mouth to pray. So when you pray make sure you mean every word you say because He's listening.

Praying should be simple, yet sincere and from the heart. You'll notice as you pray the focus will begin to shift from you to God and you'll start to feel His presence and grace all around you. I remember one day I was praying and I had gotten so deep into the prayer, that I missed my bus to campus for class. I made it to class, but I was still basking in His presence. When you get into the presence of God, it's an indescribable feeling to the point you'll want to stay there for as long as you can.

I know there are some people who've never prayed in their life or don't know how to for whatever reason, Matthew 6:9-13 gives an example of how to pray. That's the great thing about the Bible; it has answers to everything you'll need answers to. I read a post one day that said: "BIBLE…Basic Instructions Before Leaving Earth!"

Things Happen...Trust God

Glad to see you made it to the last chapter, which just happens to be the other most important chapter in the whole book. This is by far my favorite because I had to go through all those things in the previous chapters just to get to this one. I don't think I'd change anything that happened in the previous chapters because it built my character physically, mentally, emotionally and spiritually.

"But you shall receive power (ability, efficiency, and might) when the Holy Spirit has come upon you, and you shall be My witnesses..." (Acts 1:8, AMP).

In the first chapter I mentioned that we have a personal relationship with the Holy Spirit; we should also have a consuming relationship. What I mean by consuming is that you allow the Spirit to change you, to be seen through you.

There was a time when the Holy Spirit only empowered certain individuals for specific purposes. When Jesus died, his physical presence was dead so he poured out his spiritual presence so that it's power could be available to all who wanted it.

"Therefore if any man be in Christ, he is a new creature: old things are passed away; behold all things are become new" (2 Corinthians 5:17, KJV). When I read this verse, it reminds me of a butterfly and how, in the most simplistic terms; it goes from a caterpillar, through

its pupa stage and comes out as a beautiful butterfly. That's how our life should be transformed once we receive the Holy Spirit, so much more beautiful and full than before we received it.

"But the Holy Spirit produces this kind of fruit in our lives: love, joy, peace, patience, kindness, goodness, faithfulness" (Galatians 5:22, NLT). These are all of the characteristics present in Jesus Christ, we call them the "Fruit of the Spirit," and only the Spirit can bring them out of you.

Here is another version of the same verse some might find a bit more appealing. *"But what happens when we live God's way? He brings gifts into our lives, much the same way that fruit appears in an orchard—things like affection for others, exuberance about life, serenity. We develop a willingness to stick with things, a sense of compassion in the heart, and a conviction that a basic holiness permeates things and people. We find ourselves involved in loyal commitments, not needing to force our way in life, able to marshal and direct our energies wisely" (Galatians 5:22, MSG).*

I noticed that during my first two years of college, I was in the best place I could be environmentally. I was living in the dorms, I got along with my roommates, all I had to do was walk downstairs for my meals, I pretty much had no worries, but something really didn't feel right, I felt like I was missing something. Another year passed. I was in my own apartment now; I had bills now, had to cook all my meals, but I found myself with more joy then than ever before and found myself randomly singing throughout the day. I prayed for others more than I prayed for myself, not only that but I found myself praying, thanking God for Who He is rather than asking for anything. And I genuinely just woke up smiling. Those are the kind of things I saw the Spirit producing in me, and I absolutely loved it. When we grow in this fruit it results in us fulfilling the intending purpose of the law, to love God and his people.

- It's Not Easy, but It's Possible -

Living for Christ is not easy, but it's not as hard as some people make it seem. God's way of living contradicts the world's way of living. As long as you let the Spirit lead you in the direction you should go, you will always be in the Will of God. You have to realize that yes; we are flesh so we will have shortcomings and that's okay; repent, learn from it, and go on living. Becoming a Christian means beginning a new relationship with God, not just all of a sudden deciding to do things right. Becoming Christ-like is a progressive experience, which involves continually *striving* and the glory that the Spirit imparts will gradually transform you to do so. I would like to close this chapter out with a prayer.

Lord, I would first like to just simply say thank you. Thank you for just being you, for sending your son to die on the cross for our sins and not just that but for allowing us to have someone to shape our lives after. Thank you for your word that helps to guide us in our everyday life; help us to understand it, to apply it and to stand firm on it as we go throughout our life. Thank you for the person reading this book. I ask that you help them to know you better, show them your glory. Lord, we know that you give us choices, but we ask that you help us to *make the right choices in our education and life. For those who haven't received your Spirit, we ask that you open their hearts to receive it. And for those who have received your Spirit we ask that you continually help them to mature in their spiritual walk on a daily basis. Lord, we understand that everything we go through is for a reason, and we say thank you because we know whatever the reason may be, you were in the midst even if we didn't feel like it at times. You're faithful even when we aren't faithful to you. God, we know everything we'll ever need, we already possess in ourselves, so we just ask that you help to bring those things out and anything that is not like you Lord, take it out of us. Lord, help us to be the light so that others can see the light in us and help us to love others the way you love us. We've made a choice to deny this world and follow you, help us not to get distracted along the way and to not to fall back into the hands of the enemy. Lord, we know you have a bright future planned for us, and to that, again we say thank. Now, let us not be so focused on the destination that we forget to enjoy the **JOURNEY!** In Jesus' name, Amen.*

Blessings to you as you journey along in college and in life.